INSIDER'S GUIDE TO CREDIT CARDS

Second Edition

Bedford/St. Martin's   Boston   ◆   New York

Manufactured in the United States of America.

8   7   6   5   4   3
f   e   d   c   b   a

For information, write: Bedford/St. Martin's, 75 Arlington Street, Boston, MA 02116 (617-399-4000)

ISBN 978-1-4576-5382-7

Contents

iv *Contents*

INSIDER'S GUIDE TO CREDIT CARDS

Why should you read this guide? Good question. And we'll answer it with another question: You wouldn't think of taking a car out for a spin without knowing how to operate it, would you? In one major way, credit cards are a lot like cars: They can be used as a brilliant modern convenience—or an air-conditioned, well-upholstered missile.

Used properly, credit cards are a wonderful thing. Simply read this driving manual first so you'll know how to navigate credit and use it to your own advantage. Here, we'll show you how to get a credit card—if you decide you really need one—and avoid financial catastrophe. And if you've already spent yourself into a hole, we'll help you dig out of it.

A Brief History of Student Credit

Historically, students have been especially vulnerable to credit card debt. For many years, credit card lenders ran wild. They invaded college campuses, showering naïve students with credit card offers that gave them unprecedented license to spend like crazy. Consequently, many of these students graduated under the curse of insane, insurmountable debt.

But then the government decided to reclaim the youth of America. In February 2009, it stepped in with new laws designed to slow the flow of credit to students. No longer could creditors set up tables on college campuses and suck in hungry, fashion-addicted coeds with offers of free pizza and T-shirts. More important, from now on, students under age twenty-one would have to fight to get credit cards in their own names—or at least cards with spending limits above $500—unless they could show an independent and sizeable source of income. Enlisting a responsible adult cosigner (a human safety net in the form of a parent or guardian) emerged as a rampant new trend.

With order restored, students were once again free to gradually learn how to use credit in a responsible, desirable, and life-enhancing manner.

Why Starting With a Budget Is Crucial

What's the first step toward being one of those responsible, credit-card-holding students? Before you even reach for a credit card, you must put some checks in place to keep you from spending your brains out. You need to know how to manage your money. In other words, you need to create a budget.

Isn't it enough to have a vague idea of what you spend? Not a chance. Keeping track of your personal finances can be tricky, especially in college. Many students are shocked to discover how quickly incidental, day-to-day purchases can add up. And, of course, you don't want to derail your studies and have to drop out of school because you ran out of money. That's why having a solid, viable budget is essential. It will help you see where your money goes and where you can cut corners.

Steps to Create a Budget

The best part about making a budget? Once you have your records in order, it only takes a few minutes. Let's break it down:

- **Determine your sources of income,** whether this be through a job, dear ol' mom and dad, scholarships, etc. Track how much money is coming in and when.

- **Track your spending for a week or two** (or better, a full month) by recording every bill you pay and purchase you make.

- **Next, write down your estimated monthly expenses.** Use your findings from tracking your spending as a benchmark for how much you typically spend each month. Try to be ruthlessly objective when doing this. For example, if you can't go twenty-four hours without hitting Jack in the Box, don't budget $12 a month for eating out.

- **If you aren't sure how much you spend in a particular category, err on the side of caution and overestimate.**

That way you won't end up short at the end of the month. You can always tweak the numbers later.

- **Try a test run.** For the next few weeks, follow your budget, track your spending, and see if all the numbers add up. If the numbers don't add up, first check your math, then make adjustments.

You can stick to a budget and still have fun. Just factor the fun into your budget. Use the sample budget on page 5 to get started (see the completed example on page 4, too).

Cut Costs

Once you've fine-tuned your budget, you may find that you're spending three times as much as you can possibly afford. At this point you will need to do some cost cutting.

- First, identify which of your expenses are *needs* (i.e., rent, books) and which are *wants* (i.e., the latest gadgets, gourmet coffee, Fendi baguettes, that road trip to Vegas). Cut way back on the wants.

- Second, find more wallet-friendly ways to meet your needs. Move to a cheaper apartment. Furnish your new digs with finds from Craigslist and Goodwill. Split expenses with a roommate so you can pay your bills on time and avoid late fees. Sell your car and embrace biking or public transportation. Seek out student discounts as well as free concerts and sporting events. And if you need to smarten up your look, scour second-hand clothing stores.

TIP **Go mobile.** There are several easily downloadable apps for your smartphone that are designed to help you budget your money. Check out the following:

Mint. Manage your money and help with your budgeting needs. **www.mint.com**

BudgetBuster. You can track your daily, weekly, and monthly expenses. **www.tippytops.net/iphone/budgetbuster**

Figure 1: Sample Monthly Student Budget

> You can identify which categories are fixed
> expenses and which are variable expenses.
> The fixed categories—like rent, for
> example—will not change
> month to month.

Month: September	Estimated Amount	Actual Amount
Income		
Paycheck	$1,500	$1,500
Student Loans	500	500
Total Income	**+$2,000**	**+$2,000**
Expenses		
Rent	$500	$500
Heat	45	41
Electricity	50	61
Water	15	16
Cell Phone	45	50
Internet	30	30
Gas + Car Expenses	50	80
Books	250	212
Groceries	240	315
Eating Out	30	17
Entertainment	30	35
Personal Care	50	32
Clothing	50	26
Miscellaneous	50	700
Total Expenses	**−$1,435**	**−$1,485**
Savings for the month:	$565	$515

> You reach this number by
> subtracting your total
> expenses from your income.

> Note the difference between the
> two. It is highly unlikely these
> two numbers will match the first
> go-around, so you may need to
> cut costs or make other changes.

Outline Your Own Budget

Using the blank template below, outline your own monthly budget.

Month:		
	Estimated Amount	**Actual Amount**
Income		
Total Income	+$	+$
Expenses		
Total Expenses	–$	–$
Savings for the month:		

Understanding Your Risk: Pros and Cons of Credit Cards

Once you've learned the invaluable life skill of how to stick to a budget, you might feel ready to take on a credit card. But don't get too comfortable just yet! If, as a student, you run up big bills in this bold new world of cosigner credit cards, it may threaten not only your own financial future but also that of your entire family. And once you turn twenty-one—or if you're over eighteen with steady income—all bets are off: Unscrupulous creditors can pounce on you like fresh meat.

So why not study up on how to use credit in a way that brings everyone peace and fulfillment? Vive the enlightened consumer!

Good Reasons to Own a Credit Card

There are plenty of good reasons to own a credit card, and for most people it makes sense to have one. (As we've mentioned, if you're under twenty-one and want a spending limit above $500, you'll need an adult cosigner or be able to show proof that you have the means to repay your debts.) Consider the pros of using plastic:

- **It helps you establish a credit history,** making it much easier for you to get loans for a car, home, business, or more education down the road. (As a rule, the better your credit rating, the less interest you'll pay and the more money you'll save.)

- **It's helpful in an emergency** if you have a medical crisis or are stranded somewhere without a ride or plane ticket.

- **It offers some consumer protection** that you can't get by paying with cash, a check, or your debit card. For example, if you return a purchase, your account can be credited on the spot—no waiting for the store to mail you a refund.

- **It can save you money if your wallet is stolen.** Under federal law, your maximum liability for unauthorized use of your credit card is $50. If you report the loss before your credit cards are used, the issuer can't hold you responsible for any unauthorized charges.

- **It allows you to make purchases online** as well as to secure hotel and car rental reservations.

- **It's essential for traveling abroad.** Credit cards are accepted more widely than the American dollar; you can use them without having to change currency or deal with traveler's checks.

- **It might even earn you special rewards.** Many cards give you frequent flier miles, reward points, or cash back to your account in the form of rebates.

How Credit Cards Can Get You in Trouble

Credit debt is the third most common reason for personal bankruptcy in the United States (after unemployment and medical expenses), so it's critical to understand the risks that come with credit cards. The biggest risk with credit cards, particularly if you're over twenty-one and can get a high spending limit without a cosigner, is that they can tempt you to spend more than you can afford. It can pay to walk on the wild side—but not if you're running a tab. Misuse just one credit card and . . .

- **It could wreck your credit rating, making it hard to get loans and financial aid in the future.** A bad credit score can take decades to escape. To make matters worse, it can even count against you when you're job-hunting: Employers often run credit checks on prospective hires.

- **It may cause your grades to suffer,** since you'll be forced to work more hours to pay down your bill.

- **It can hinder your options after you graduate.** If you are carrying a lot of debt, you've got only three options when you begin to support yourself: (1) land a job with a big salary; (2) join a socialist commune; or (3) stay home every night, living on peanut butter and Ramen noodles, while paying off both your student loans and your credit card bill.

- **It adds pressure to the already stressful life of a college student.** Some students get in so deep, they have to drop out of school in order to work full-time. Others are forced to declare bankruptcy—a hideous ordeal that ranks up there with divorce and the death of a family member in the anxiety department.

Getting the wrong kind of credit card can have some nasty consequences, too. You don't want to be caught off-guard by overdraft charges or a letter telling you that your interest rate will triple in the next six weeks.

Debit Cards: A Safer Bet Than Using Credit?

In most cases, a debit card is safer than a credit card. A debit or ATM card lets you buy things at grocery stores, retail shops, and gas stations. On many campuses, students can also fund the card to pay for meals in the dining hall and other school services. Unlike a credit card, a debit card instantly deducts the cost of your purchase from your checking account. It's like a check that's processed in the blink of an eye—the equivalent of paying cash.

Advantages:

- **A debit card is PIN-code protected.** Credit cards aren't.

- **It carries no interest fees.**

- **It saves you from having to carry cash.**

- **It limits your expenses to the balance of your checking account.**

Disadvantages:

- **It's easy to spend down your checking account** on random stuff and suddenly find you have no rent money.

- **Using your debit card for purchases *does not* offer all the consumer protections you get with a credit card.** Case in point: If your debit card is lost or stolen, you might be liable for more unauthorized deductions than you would be with

---

TIP Get your debit card through Visa or MasterCard. They offer a zero liability policy for debit-card fraud on all debit cards that bear their logos—regardless of how long you take to report the incident.

a credit card. Even worse, you might not realize for hours or days that your debit card is missing—at which point the thief could have already cleaned out your checking account.

- **Under the Electronic Fund Transfer Act,** as long as you report your card stolen within two days, you won't lose more than $50 of the money that was stolen. Wait longer than that and you could be liable for as much as $500. Beyond sixty days, you may not have any loss protection at all.

- **Many banks charge you to use their ATMs if you don't have an account with them.** You may have to pay a surcharge of 10 percent or even more.

Getting In Gear: How To Decide If You *Need* a Credit Card

If at this point you haven't been scared away by the horror stories, it's time for some honest self-assessment: Is a credit card a good option for you? Here's how to find out.

Make Sure You Need It for a Good Reason

Why do you want a credit card? Is it for regular, legitimate expenses or for emergencies? Or, be truthful here, to keep up with your well-heeled classmates? Many students find themselves wanting to live like their new friends, throwing frugality to the wind. Want to treat everyone to a round of beers at the pub? Get the latest and greatest smartphone just like your study partner? Plastic can make it all happen . . . and then you get the heart-stopping bill.

There **are two acceptable reasons to get a credit card** (provided you have the money to pay it off at the end of each month):

- To conveniently pay for regular expenses like textbooks, phone bills, and utilities

- To have one just for emergencies

Then there are the following slippery, potentially hazardous, reasons to get a credit card that you need to discuss with a credit counselor in your school's financial aid office—and your cosigner should you have or need one:

- To try to cover your tuition or bridge a gap in your current financial aid

- To supplement your cash flow while you're working part-time in a low-paying job

- To access money that you are planning to pay back over the summer or that you may need to help your family get by during a tough economic period

Chances are, there are cheaper and safer ways to accomplish these goals.

Know How Much Debt You Can Afford

In case we haven't said this enough already, figuring out how much credit you should have is essential. The danger of having too little is that you could go over your limit and incur penalty fees. Most student credit cards have a sensible $500 spending cap. But once you turn twenty-one, having too much credit becomes a much bigger danger since you could be tempted to spend beyond your means. We suggest taking this simple test:

- Look at your income and liquid assets. Do you have enough money so you can pay off the balance of your credit card each month? YES _____ NO _____

- How responsible are you about managing your money? Do you usually pay your debts promptly? YES _____ NO _____

- Do you have a clear understanding of why you want the credit card and what you'll use it for? YES _____ NO _____

- Are you good at setting and keeping within spending limits? YES _____ NO _____

- Do you have a monthly budget? YES _____ NO _____

If you can't honestly answer "yes" to these questions, you should avoid credit cards completely or get one with only the lowest credit limit possible (and make sure you stay below that threshold). Having a credit card available for emergencies, such as travel reservations and vital online purchases, makes sense, but only if it has a cap to keep you from going broke.

Think Like the Credit Card Companies

Before you open your umpteenth student credit card offer, ask yourself: "Why do credit card companies love students so much? Why is it so insanely easy for a low-income bookworm like me to get credit?"

First, college students represent fresh blood—a market that isn't already maxed out on credit and can be locked in for a lifetime of brand loyalty. Second, college graduates tend to land higher-paying jobs than high school grads, so your card issuer could benefit down the road. Third, marketing to students is cheap: All those flyers you get at the bookstore cost next to nothing. Plus, the college student market constantly replenishes itself with new first-year and transfer students.

The more insidious issue: You're a vulnerable target. While some students have experience managing their own finances, those who don't can be naïve about the cost of borrowing. For unscrupulous card issuers, such inexperience makes students sitting ducks. Trust us, these greedy predators don't give a hoot about your or your classmates' financial futures. They'll enjoy tricking you into debt. They'll laugh cruelly as you fill their pockets with soul-crushing interest and penalty fees.

Sure we sound harsh. But to psych yourself up enough to want to study up on credit and become an enlightened consumer, you need to glimpse the real enemy here.

Don't Assume You're the Exception

From undergrads to MBA candidates, students of all types have been known to spend themselves into a hole before graduation. You'd be amazed at how easy it is to get approved for a handful of credit cards and quickly max them out on pizza, clothes, video games, and music downloads. Small, non-vital purchases have a nasty way of snowballing. Let's review the statistics. According to a 2009 study by the student-loan giant Sallie Mae:

- Eighty-four percent of undergraduate students have at least one credit card.

- The average undergraduate student carries $3,173 in credit card debt.

- Ninety-two percent of graduate students have at least one credit card.

- The average graduate student carries $8,612 in credit card debt.

And that's on top of the tens of thousands of dollars the average student already owes in educational loans.

Don't Get Hooked by Flattery

You might think that getting a credit card solicitation from a bank or retailer represents a mark of status. Actually, whenever a "You've been specially chosen for this exclusive offer!" letter arrives in the mail, you can bet that it's been sent out to millions of other people, too—lots of whom have terrible credit and are likely to default. Pre-approved? That doesn't mean anything either. You won't get a special rate or break when it comes to the terms and costs of the deal. And the small print generally gives your card company the right to change the deal you were preapproved for.

It's a Lenders' World. Learn Their Lingo

We get it. You don't *want* to read all the dry financial terms that credit issuers like to keep shrouded in mystery. But mastering the terminology is crucial: You'll find lots of important stuff—and sometimes, booby traps—buried in the fine print.

To motivate yourself, think about all of the greedy, unprincipled lenders out there and how they'd love to spend the next few decades wringing you dry of all blood, sweat, and tears. Feel stronger? Okay, let's begin.

> **TIP** **Shred it.** When you do get those unsolicited credit card offers in the mail (and you will), be sure to shred them before you throw them in the trash. They contain personal information that you'll want to keep out of strangers' hands.

The Big Three

In order to understand credit terminology, three terms are particularly important. Here they are, along with their definitions and some additional information you'll need to know.

Annual fees.

- *Definition:* This is the amount of money the issuer will charge to your account every year for the privilege of having the card.

- *Must-know info:* Avoid cards with annual fees and cards that waive the fee for only the first year. (The exception: In cases where you—against our advice—intend to carry a balance, you might want a card with an annual fee. It could offer substantially lower rates.)

Interest rate (a.k.a. finance charge).

- *Definition:* The interest rate is the percentage of the loan amount that the issuer charges you to borrow money. In short, any unpaid balance on your card at the end of the month becomes a loan, and the credit card company will charge you interest on that loan. That interest compounds on a monthly basis. (See **Compounding interest,** on the next page.)

- *Must-know info:* When it comes to interest rates, most experts say that it's better to have a low, fixed-rate credit card than a low, variable-rate credit card. Why should that be? Card companies can raise the finance charges on fixed-rate cards when interest rates go up, but the change isn't automatic and they need to give you fifteen days' notice. With a variable-rate card, your rate can bounce around regularly and without notice.

> **TIP** **Don't plan to rely on your card as a source of cash advances.** You should get them only when absolutely necessary. Why? Cash advances usually carry a higher interest rate, and interest accrues from the moment the money is withdrawn. It's an expensive way to borrow money.

TIP **Know the facts.** If you're tempted by a teaser rate, it's crucial to study the literature and find out exactly when and by how much the rate could increase. While not all teaser rate offers are a bad deal, reading the fine print protects you from the ones that are. Note: New laws require creditors to give consumers forty-five days' advance notice of significant changes to their card terms.

Annual Percentage Rate (APR).

- *Definition:* The APR is a more accurate representation of the cost of borrowing from a credit card. It includes all interest charges (including the interest rate you'll pay if you carry a balance, take out a cash advance, or transfer a balance from another card), plus any annual fees or other costs, and then calculates all of these charges as a yearly percentage of the loan amount.

- *Must-know info:* A single credit card may have several APRs—one APR for purchases, another for cash advances, and yet another for balance transfers from another card. The APRs for cash advances generally run the highest (e.g., 17.8 percent for purchases or balance transfers, and 22.9 percent for cash advances).

Common Traps

Credit card holders beware! Understand the common traps associated with the terms below so you can steer clear of financial misfortune.

Teaser rate.

- *Definition:* A teaser is a very low interest rate offered for a short period of time to attract you to the card.

- *Must-know info:* Teaser rates may sound good at first, but they're not always as great as they seem. For instance, a company may offer you a zero-interest card or a card with a low introductory rate of 2.9 percent for three months. After three months, the rate will increase dramatically—leaving you stuck with a very expensive card. Or your fantastic rate might triple the first time you're late with a payment. Most people are better off with a modest, fixed rate that stays consistent over the long haul.

Compounding interest.

- *Definition:* When you make only low or minimum monthly payments, interest continues to accumulate, making the cost of borrowing higher. This is the compounding effect. By the second month that you don't pay off your card, you'll be paying interest on the higher balance, which already includes one month of interest charges. And so on.

- *Must-know info:* This compounding effect can accumulate quickly—particularly if you have a high rate of interest, which student credit cards often do. For example, let's say you owe $2,820 on your credit card and have an annual interest rate of 15 percent, which is typical for student credit cards. If you make the typical minimum payment—percent of balance, plus interest and fees—you'll be debt-free in . . . twenty-one years!

Penalties (a.k.a. over-the-limit fees).

- *Definition:* These are fees that result from not paying your bill on time, paying too little of it, closing your account before an agreed-upon date, or charging more than your credit limit allows (an overdraft).

- *Must-know info:* While the government is cracking down on the most outrageous fees, there are still dozens of potential penalties attached to credit cards. You may not be able to learn

---

TIP **Always ask to opt out of overdraft service.** Otherwise, even if you don't have enough credit left in your account for a transaction, the bank may still allow it to proceed. You might not even realize that you're overdrawn or that you've incurred a penalty until your bill arrives. The average overdraft fee is $27 per transaction. See where this is going?

the ins and outs of all of them, but be aware of the ones most likely to affect you. Penalties can run as high as $50, which throws your APR into a whole new league.

Other Basics

To fully build your credit card vocabulary, get to know these additional terms.

Credit limit.

- *Definition:* This is how much you're able to charge.

- *Must-know info:* You may have a credit limit that's fairly low to start (about $500). But once you turn twenty-one (or if you're between the ages of eighteen and twenty and have a cosigner who agrees to the plan), your issuer is likely to raise that limit. It sounds terrific. But believe us, it's not. Remember, just because your credit card company is willing to give you more credit doesn't mean you should use it: Odds are, you can't actually afford that much debt.

Grace period.

- *Definition:* This is how long something can stay on your bill before you're charged interest.

- *Must-know info:* For initial purchases, your grace period may be twenty to thirty days. But there's no grace period on balances carried over from the previous month. They accrue interest daily.

Billing cycle.

- *Definition:* The number of days between bills.

- *Must-know info:* Bills won't necessarily come once a month. Under new legislation, creditors can give you as little as twenty-one days to pay your bills. (While it sounds counterintuitive, this is actually good news; some billing cycles used to be as short as two weeks!)

> **TIP** **Pay attention to your payment due date.** This is the date that your payment has to be recorded in your card issuer's computer system, not the day it's postmarked or arrives at the company's offices. To avoid a late fee, mail payments in several days early or pay your bill online.

Minimum payment.

- *Definition:* The minimum amount a cardholder can pay to keep the account from going into default.

- *Must-know info:* Beware getting in the habit of paying only the minimum balance each month. See Compounding interest (page 15).

The Balance Calculation Method

The interest rate or finance charge is the dollar amount you pay to use credit. The amount depends on your outstanding balance and the APR. So here's the thing: Credit card companies use one of several methods to calculate your outstanding balance. And the method can make a big difference in the finance charge you'll pay.

Your outstanding balance may be calculated

- over one billing cycle or two;
- using the adjusted balance, the average daily balance, or your previous balance; and
- including or excluding new purchases in the balance.

Depending on the balance you carry and the timing of your purchases and payments, you'll usually have a lower finance charge with one-cycle billing and either the average daily balance method excluding new purchases, the adjusted balance method, or the previous balance method.

If you don't understand how your balance is calculated, ask your card company to explain it to you. Also, the Federal Reserve Web site offers detailed information about balance calculation methods in plain English: **federalreserve.gov.**

The Rules of Shopping for a Credit Card

Follow this advice, whether you're getting your first credit card or your fifth . . .

1. **Choose carefully.** Don't sign up for the first offer you get. There are hundreds of offers out there, so it pays to be picky. Consider your lifestyle and paying habits (the real-life vs. fantasy version). Make a list of the most important features you need in a card and shop accordingly. Start online. **Kiplinger.com** will help you match a credit card deal to your specific needs and habits. The FDIC (Federal Deposit Insurance Corporation, at **fdic.gov**) also offers expert advice on choosing and using credit.

2. **One major credit card that's accepted worldwide is all you really need.** This means Visa, MasterCard, or American Express. Be aware, however, that American Express tends to charge an annual fee for its cards and is not as widely accepted as Visa and MasterCard. Also, all American Express cards are not created equal: The company offers many card types, including (a) the expense-account kind that you must pay off completely at the end of each month, and (b) an Optima card, which works like a MasterCard or Visa and lets you carry a balance from one month to the next.

    *   *We recommend against getting a retailer's card*—the kind that comes from Macy's, Sears, or Gap. That kind of credit is easy to get and the store usually offers a discount on your first purchase when you apply. But such cards limit your buying power to a specific chain and usually carry a higher interest rate than a good Visa or MasterCard.

TIP **The Reward programs.** What if a credit card offers special rewards or rebates that you find essential? Beware that these perks come with a hidden cost. Usually the card has a slightly higher interest rate. Yet that's not necessarily a deal killer. As long as you don't intend to carry a balance on the card, it might be a perfectly fine choice.

> **TIP** **Don't apply for too many cards or close accounts frequently.** Forget how many freebies come with a new application offer. The best way to get a healthy credit score is to grow credit slowly. Each time you apply for credit, a credit inquiry appears on your credit report and hangs around for two years. Lots of inquiries hurt your credit score.

- *While we're at it, you probably don't need a gas-company card either.* Now that all gas stations accept debit cards and most all major credit cards, having a gas card doesn't make much sense.

3. **Aim for the lowest interest rate you can get.** In 2009, student interest rates hovered fairly high—around 15 percent. If you don't count introductory rates, actual interest rates average even higher. Use a simple Web search to learn what a card's interest rates are before you accept it. You can easily calculate the cost of borrowing using an online interest calculator such as the one run by CNN or Money magazine at **money.cnn.com/tools/debtplanner/debtplanner.jsp.**

The exception? If you know that despite your best efforts, you might be late a few times with the payment, use a calculator to see if a card with a slightly higher interest rate but lower late fee might be a better deal.

4. **Remember to ask for a low credit limit and no overdraft service.** That's the best long-term strategy. It lets you build good credit rating and avoid debt at the same time.

5. **Once you narrow in on an offer, examine it very closely and look for their hooks.** Web sites like **Bankrate.com,** **CreditCards.com,** and **CreditMe.com** not only help you comparison shop for credit card rates, but also offer advice on how to sniff out a scam. (Bankrate even includes a list of the twenty most common traps set by conniving card companies.) A few quick strokes of the keyboard and you'll know whether your offer is a good deal or a classic consumer nightmare.

6. **Rule out surprises.** Under what circumstances can the card company change your interest rate or any other terms of the deal? The APR may increase if you are late in making payments. Even a small rise in the APR can make a big difference in how much you'll pay over a year.

7. **Negotiate.** This is the fun part. What's negotiable when it comes to credit cards? Everything! Do you like the credit limit but not the billing cycle? Ask for a longer period between bills. Did you discover that the grace period is incredibly short? Ask for a longer one. Have you been carrying a balance for a while on a high-interest card? Call the company and ask for a better rate.

   Credit card companies know that once they lose your business, it's an uphill battle to get it back. That's the reason they're often willing to negotiate with you, even years down the road. Simply put, it's cheaper than having to replace you with a new customer.

How to Protect Your Account Information

OK, so you have a credit card. Now it's time to protect your account information:

- Sign the back of your card immediately and be sure to shred your statements before you toss them in the trash or recycling bin.

- Don't leave your card or receipts lying around.

- In case your card gets lost or stolen, write down the card number, its expiration date, and the contact details of your card issuer and file the information in a safe place.

TIP **Get a copy of your credit report.** Everyone is entitled to one free credit report a year from each of the three major credit bureaus. Make sure to order yours from the U.S. government Web site, **annualcreditreport.com**. Sites offering "free" credit reports usually require paid memberships for additional credit products. So save your money. Use it to pay your bills instead!

- Notify your card company in advance if you're moving so your statement doesn't end up at your old address. (Better yet, ask for online bills.)

- *Never, ever give your credit card number to strangers* who call or e-mail you, no matter how legitimate they seem. Bogus e-mails currently rank as the biggest scam on the Internet. The crooks behind them are hard to catch.

- Always monitor your statements closely. Check new charges and any miscellaneous fees. If you see something you don't recognize, call your cosigner, if you have one, and your credit card company and ask for an explanation.

- Keep tabs on your credit report. Regularly reviewing your credit history pays off in major ways. First, it alerts you to identity theft—an insidious and increasingly common crime in which someone assumes your identity, secretly opens up accounts in your name, and has the bills sent to another address. Second, you'll be able to check for inaccuracies: payments not credited or another mix-up that the credit bureau needs to fix. Third, you can catch unauthorized activity on accounts that you've closed or haven't used lately.

What to Do if You Think You Might be Slipping Into Debt

If you suspect that you're slipping into debt, you're not alone. It's easy to get in over your head with credit. In fact, more than half of Americans don't pay off their credit cards every month. So remember to watch for these red flags:

Slippery ground

- Carrying a balance on your card(s) every month

- Spending money you don't have with the expectation that money's on the way

- Paying for basics—like tuition or groceries—with a credit card

- Not having a budget (A classic don't. You should always take care to prioritize what you need and keep an eye on where your money is going.)

Major danger

- Using a student loan to pay down a credit card
- Having to sell personal assets (stocks or possessions) to pay a credit card bill
- Working more hours or during vacations to pay off debts
- Getting into a cycle of working to pay back money rather than save it
- Holding several cards, each carrying a balance
- Making only the minimum payment on a balance
- Ignoring creditors
- Keeping your debt a secret from your parents and friends

Online Banking

Online banking allows customers to access their account through a secure Web site created by the bank. With online banking, it is becoming easier to pay your bills online and view account information from your smartphone or computer without ever having to set foot in a bank. In this increasing digital world, here are some ways in which you can make online banking work for you:

- **You can conveniently initiate transactions online,** such as a transfer, a withdrawal request, or a bill payment, in a matter of minutes.
- **You can set up alerts** so the bank will let you know when your balance is low.
- **With Automatic Bill Pay, you can set up your account so you never miss a deadline.** All you have to worry about is making sure the money is in your account.
- **There is less paper mail such as bank statements,** which will decrease the amount of paper lying around susceptible to identity theft and results in less shredding projects for you. Win, win.

Stage 1 Defcon Alert

- **Missing payments.** Skipping a payment is worse than paying the minimum. The interest compounds, and a black mark "thirty-days late" appears on your credit report. Missed payments linger there for seven years, dragging your credit rating into the basement.

- **Paying bills late.** Even if your credit card is paid faithfully, the issuer can opt to hike your interest rate if you make late payments on other bills such as car loans, utility bills, and other credit cards. This is called universal default.

- **Using cash advances to pay other credit cards.** The credit card shuffle—where you take out a cash advance on one card to pay for another—is extremely costly and a sure sign that you're in over your head.

- **Having to consider leaving school to work full-time to pay off debt.**

You've Spent Yourself Into a Hole. Now What?

If you recognize yourself in any of the aforementioned warning signs, you're probably in some trouble already. But even if you aren't overextended, following some simple credit practices will help you keep your head above water. Here are some useful tricks:

- **Use your debit card instead of a credit card whenever possible.** But don't drain your checking account. If you do, you may have to get a cash advance to cover rent and other essentials.

- **Don't keep more than one or two credit cards.**

- **If you have more than two cards**, get rid of those with the highest interest rates and harshest penalties preferably by paying them off or, if you can't do that, by moving the balance to a new, low-interest card. Then cancel and cut up the old cards.

- **Keep your family in the loop.** You might need them to bail you out financially. Plus, you'll want their support when you're down. A lot of borrowers get into trouble because they're too afraid to ask for help.

- **Avoid impulse shopping.** Before you hit the stores, draw up a detailed list of everything you need—along with what you can afford to spend—and follow it religiously. Also, have a snack: Psychologists have found that when you're hungry, you're more likely to buy more of everything—not just food. Lastly, deal in cash: Studies show that handing over your hard-earned bills hurts more than paying with plastic, making you less likely to overspend.

- **Maintain a good relationship with your financial aid office** and seek out free credit counseling if you suspect or know you have a problem. A credit counselor can help you consolidate and manage debts—and avoid the torments of personal bankruptcy—until you're back on your feet again. You can find one through your campus business office.

- **After you graduate,** ask your lender for a lower APR. Students tend to pay higher interest rates, so you can probably negotiate a better deal.

Insider Tactics ‖ How Top Students Manage Their Credit

The Planner *Alan Levy*

Chemical & biomolecular engineering major in Pennsylvania

"The whole online banking thing is beautiful because I can check my balance anytime. I have an app for my bank on my smartphone—that makes it easy."

TIP **Beware the do-gooder impulse.** Are you over twenty-one and wrestling with the idea of using your credit to support a family member or friend? It's a noble impulse, but the truth is, don't do it. Think about it: By cosigning for other people, you make yourself liable for any unpaid balances they run up and you could easily find yourself bogged down with more debt than you can afford to repay. Bottom line: Talk with a credit counselor about your options. There may be smarter ways to help.

- **Use parental support as a launch pad.** "I have a checking account that my parents put money in, and a credit card linked to that account. At some point after I graduate, I'll be the one who's putting money in the account, so it will be a credit card I'll keep forever. And in the meantime, I'm building up my credit."

- **Start saving early on.** "I've already linked a savings account to my checking account. I can check that balance online, too."

- **Divide and conquer.** "My parents and I worked out a budget together and they send me a monthly allowance. It's easy for me to manage because I split what I get into four weeks. If I overspend a little the first week, I'll just cut back the next week or two till I'm back on track."

The Improviser *Doug Witt*

Nursing major in Arizona

"Now that I'm in college, I depend on my credit card quite a bit. Even though I work fifteen hours a week and the pay is good, it's really hard to make ends meet, especially around finals if I cut back my work hours to study. So once the well runs dry in my checking account, the credit card comes out."

- **Embrace the frugal summer.** "I'm not 100 percent depending on student loans, so most of my money goes to tuition. My plan is simple: I work all year, but when the semester ends I try to work even more hours. That way I can pay off my credit card balance completely, and build up as big a surplus as possible."

- **Start with a low ceiling.** "I've got a $2,500 credit limit. My balance usually stays really low, though one time it climbed to $2,400: I got engaged and that process was expensive. It was well worth it in the end, but it took forever to pay off."

- **Check your statement obsessively**—even the stuff in the envelope that looks like boring ads. "Your card company might spring an interest-rate hike on you, in which case you can call and ask to have the original rate put back. My dad taught me that trick. It actually works!"

The Holdout *Sarah Scruby*

Music major in Florida

"I'm not old enough to have my own credit card, so my father lets me keep one on his account for necessities. Our system works well: The bills get sent home so I don't have to worry about them, and he knows I won't make wild expenditures. I don't want to abuse poor Dad."

- **Set strict priorities.** "I only pull out the credit card for things I need, not things I want. Textbooks, gas, musical supplies. Those are the essentials."

- **Don't use your credit card for food.** "It just adds up and then you lose track of what you bought."

- **Carry cash and a debit card at all times.** "That really works for me. If my credit card stays in reserve at the back of my wallet, I'll resist the urge to use it."

Helpful Resources

annualcreditreport.com

bankrate.com

Budget Planning and Budgeting Lessons   **moneyinstructor.com/budgeting.asp**

Budget Wizard   **www.cashcourse.org**

CNN/*Money* magazine   **www.money.cnn.com**

creditcardguide.com

creditcards.com

Do You Owe Me Money?   **youngmoney.com/money_management/budgeting/58**

FastWeb.com

FDIC (Federal Deposit Insurance Corporation)   **fdic.gov**

Federal Reserve Bank   **federalreserve.gov**

Financial Education   **www.educationcents.org**

Financial IQ   **mygreatlakes.org/borrower/fiq/home.html**

Free Application for Federal Student Aid   **fafsa.ed.gov**

kiplinger.com

mymoney.gov

NellieMae.com

One for Your Money   **higherone.com/oneforyourmoney**

Online Budget   **mint.com**

Three Money Lessons That Will Make You Rich   **youngmoney**
.com/money_management/savings/060929

Bibliography

Aycock, Jason. "Top 10 Ways Students Ruin Their Credit." *Creditcards*.com. CreditCards.com, n.d. Web. 15 Nov. 2009 <**www.CreditCards.com/ credit-card-news/top-10-ways-students-ruin-credit-1279.php**>.

Banjo, Shelly, "Tackle Credit Cards Now." *Finance.yahoo.com.* The Wall Street Journal Online, 22 June 2008. Web. 16 Nov. 2009 <**http:// finance.yahoo.com/banking-budgeting/article/ 105318/Tackle -Credit-Cards-Now**>.

Barrett, William P. "College Students Face New Credit Card Cut-Off." *Forbes.com.* Forbes.com, 4 Aug. 2009. Web. 15 Nov. 2009 <**www .forbes.com/2009/08/04/credit-card-reform-bill-college-stu- dents-personal-finance-collegecredit.html**>.

Braitman, Ellen. *Dollars and Sense for College Students.* New York: Random House, 1998.

"Chapter 1: Match Card and Lifestyle." *Bankrate.com.* Bankrate, Inc., n.d. Web. 15 Nov. 2009 <**www.BankRate.com/brm/green/cc/ basics1-intro.asp?caret=46**>.

"Choosing a Credit Card." *federalreserve.gov.* The Federal Reserve Board, 25 Sept. 2008. Web. 16 Nov. 2009 <**www.federalreserve .gov/Pubs/shop/**>.

"Credit Card Tips for Every Stage of Life." General Electric Credit Union. n.p. n.d. <**www.gecreditunion.org/products/Credit _Card_Tips.html**>.

Editorial. "The College Credit Card Trap." *nytimes.com.* The New York Times Company, 17 Oct. 2008. Web. 15 Nov. 2009 <**www .NYTimes.com/2008/10/18/opinion/18sat2.html**>.

"Five Reasons to Check Your Credit Report Regularly" *talewins.com.* n.p. n.d. Web. 16 Nov. 2009. <**www.talewins.com/bargains/ 5reasons.htm**>.

Gardner, John N. and Betsy O. Barefoot. "Managing Your Money." In *Your College Experience: Strategies for Success,* 10th edition. Boston, MA: Bedford/St. Martin's, 2012.

Keegan, Matthew C. "Card Issuers Scale Back on Student Credit Cards." Saycampuslife.com. SayCampusLife, 12 Aug. 2009. Web. 15 Nov. 2009 <**www.saycampuslife.com/2009/08/ 12/card-issuers-scale-back-on-student-credit-cards/**>.

Manning, Robert D. *Credit Card Nation.* New York: Basic Books, 2000.

McNaughton, Deborah. *The Insider's Guide to Managing Your Credit.* Chicago: Dearborn Financial Publishing, 1998.

"New Legislation's Effects on Student Credit." *Credit.com.* Credit .com, 19 Aug. 2009. Web. 15 Nov. 2009 <**www.credit.com/news/ credit-debt/2009-08-19/new-legislations-effects-on-student-credit.htm**>.

Prater, Connie. "Obama Signs Credit Card Reforms into Law." *Creditcards.com.* CreditCards.com, n.d. Web. 15 Nov. 2009 <**www .creditcards.com/credit-card-news/obama-signs-credit-card-law-1282.php**>.

"Student Credit Card Tips." *creditcardguide.com.* Creditcardguide. com, n.d. Web. 16 November 2009 <**www.creditcardguide.com/ student_cards.html**>.

"Skimming and Scamming: How to Protect Yourself Against Debit Card Fraud." *aba.com.* American Bankers Association, n.d. Web. 16 Nov. 2009 <**www.aba.com/ABAEF/debitcardfraud.htm**>.

Strong, Howard. *What Every Credit Card User Needs to Know.* New York: Henry Holt and Company, 1999.

Taylor, Don. "Using Zero-Percent Credit Card Offers." *Bankrate.com.* Bankrate, Inc., n.d. Web. 15 Nov. 2009 <**www.BankRate.com/ brm/news/drdon/20050815a1.asp**>.

Walker, Rob. "A For-Credit Course." *nytimes.com.* The New York Times Company. 30 Sept. 2007. Web. 15 Nov. 2009 <**www.NYTimes .com/2007/09/30/magazine/30wwln-consumed-t .html?fta=y**>.